Not won
THE LOTTERY
yet then?

GW00746395

IDEAS UNLIMITED (PUBLISHING)

Published by:
Ideas Unlimited (Publishing)
P.O. Box 125, Portsmouth
Hampshire PO1 4PP

ISBN: 1 871964 15 6

Printed & Bound in Great Britain.

This book is dedicated to
the most desperate national lottery
jackpot winner to be.

ACKNOWLEDGEMENTS

We wish to thank everyone who contributed and helped in the production of this book, in particular Liz Garrad, whose insight into this popular subject and the excellent way it is presented through her unique brand of humour, was as a result of comprehensive and painstaking research conducted in a number of unusual locations such as her local pub.

Our gratitude also goes to Willy Sanker for his magnificent cartoons, which bring the book to life.

Our thanks also goes to Michael Walsh for his clever limericks on the subject.

John Hill and Bob Crabtree for the amusing chart, and the diary pages.

Finally we wish to thank all those who supported us by buying the predecessor of this book, "HOW TO WIN THE NATIONAL LOTTERY", and making it a big success. It is through your support, and public demand that we present the sequel, which we hope you will also enjoy.

INTRODUCTION

When the National Lottery started back on November 19th 1994, no one in their wildest dreams thought that it would be as successful as it has proved to be. Jackpots of £3 Million were talked about for the initial few weeks, reducing gradually to a steady £1 Million thereafter. We have had an average of £ 8 Million jackpot continuously every week since the lottery started.

With big Jackpots and more public interest, comes more disappointments and even serious heartache. We all fantasise about winning the jackpot; but for some the fantasy is so clear and life like, spending every penny of the winnings; that when the actual dreaded draw comes, they are left once again with their dreams in shatters.

Perhaps the only consolation we can offer, is that you are one of millions of disappointed punters, and in any case as you go through this book. you will learn that may be winning the jackpot is not all its turned out to be, and you might try other alternatives..

Whatever you decide to do......GOOD LUCK!

CONTENTS

CONTENTS

WINNING THE NATIONAL LOTTERY JACKPOT

Don't just sit there dreaming of luxury and wealth
of drinking so much bubbly that you compromise your health
if you want loads of money then you may not have to nick it
just get yourself down to the shops and buy a lottery ticket.
They're drawing it tonight it's true you could be rich I swear
in some unsuspecting household sits a future millionaire
You could tell your boss on Monday stick it where the sun don't shine
But just a word of warning should your riches bring you strife
there's always those who're prone to say, "It wouldn't change my life"
"We're happy in our little place – we don't need much you see."
Well if that's true here's my advice – Please give it to me.

IF AT FIRST YOU DON'T SUCCEED.......

So you haven't won it yet then, let's be honest if you had come up on the jackpot you wouldn't need this book, and if I had come up with the jackpot I wouldn't need to write it. But since you haven't, and I do, then what is the next step to success?

What can I do to stop you sitting on the edge of your settee every Saturday night crossing your fingers and begging the fates to be kind to you?

Well I could come round and smash your telly, but apparently they broadcast it on the radio as well; and since I'm not prepared to spend my weekends destroying your electrical appliances, that's not much use. So how about cheating? No sorry, sadly Camelot have got that one sewn up as well. They must have employed the best criminal minds to come up with every scam in the book, and found a way round every one of them . . . dammit.

They are so diligent in fact that some poor chap phoned a couple of Sundays ago to claim the jackpot only to find that the Police were round sharpish to bang him up for fraud. This is what happened......
He went out with his mates on the Saturday night, therefore missing the draw on television. His mates then took his original ticket without his knowledge and swapped it with one bought early Sunday morning bearing the previous nights winning numbers; and in his hungover state he didn't check the date – Well would you???

CASH IN ON OTHERS GOOD FORTUNE

If your mother-in-law's vital statistics (Ugh), the dog's birthday and every number of every house you have ever lived in have not yet won you the lottery, then perhaps it is time to cash in on someone else's good fortune,

There is absolutely nothing wrong with riding on somebody else's coat tails, as long as you are getting a few quid into the bargain.

Take for instance the guy who won Eighteen million, and wished to remain anonymous, well fair enough, but the tabloids were hungry for a story. The rest of us were desperate to know what the lucky bloke looked like. (So we could chat him up at the next opportunity), but the poor guy didn't want to know. Did he get his wish? Did he heck. Every Tom, Dick and Malcolm was on his case eager to identify him and sell their findings to the tabloids; or at the very least get a large pay off for keeping quiet. I know I did, and why not!!!

If you are not one of the lucky Jackpot Winners, you may find this hard to understand; but it is extremely difficult to try and carry on with your normal day to day life, and hide from the public or pretend that you are not the winner. Your actions will always give you away; it is as if there is a dreaded finger pointing you out to everyone around.

IT'S HIM!!!!

CASH IN ON OTHERS GOOD FORTUNE

CASH IN ON OTHER'S GOOD FORTUNE

Alternatively, you could find out who has won and sleep with them. "Oh I couldn't do that" I hear you cry. "It wouldn't be fair". On whom would it not be fair? Well the fortunate lottery winner may well be very flattered and appreciative of your attentions and not mind in the least. You on the other hand would be doing very well, thank you, out of the deal. In fact the only cloud that one can envisage on the horizon is if you already had a partner who chose to be jealous of your behaviour.

If this turned out to be the case, then my advice is to be tolerant, and if they still object, then tell them to get lost and find a lottery winner of their own to sleep with.

This must be the very last resort. As you go through this book, you will realise that there are much better and easier ways of getting rich.

You must always remember that the only obstacle you need to get over is synchronising with those most important six balls. The charts on the following two pages, will help you understand your goals, and the steps you need to take to acquire them.

MEN USED TO DREAM ABOUT THEM - NOW WOMEN DO, TOO.

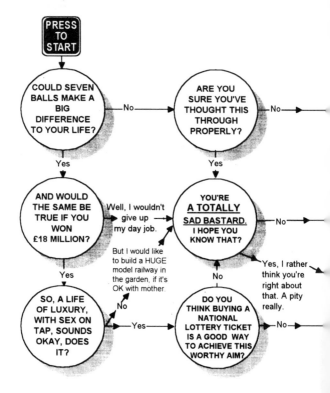

PRESS TO START

COULD SEVEN BALLS MAKE A BIG DIFFERENCE TO YOUR LIFE? —No— ARE YOU SURE YOU'VE THOUGHT THIS THROUGH PROPERLY? —No—

Yes

Yes

AND WOULD THE SAME BE TRUE IF YOU WON £18 MILLION?

Well, I wouldn't give up my day job.

But I would like to build a HUGE model railway in the garden, if it's OK with mother.

YOU'RE **A TOTALLY SAD BASTARD.** I HOPE YOU KNOW THAT? —No—

Yes, I rather think you're right about that. A pity really.

Yes

SO, A LIFE OF LUXURY, WITH SEX ON TAP, SOUNDS OKAY, DOES IT?

No

Yes

No

DO YOU THINK BUYING A NATIONAL LOTTERY TICKET IS A GOOD WAY TO ACHIEVE THIS WORTHY AIM? —No—

YES, WE'RE TALKING...

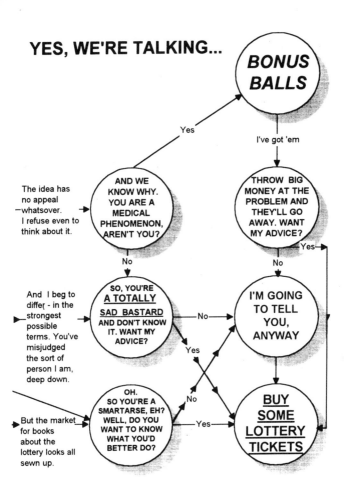

BONUS BALLS

The idea has no appeal —whatsover. I refuse even to think about it.

AND WE KNOW WHY. YOU ARE A MEDICAL PHENOMENON, AREN'T YOU?

THROW BIG MONEY AT THE PROBLEM AND THEY'LL GO AWAY. WANT MY ADVICE?

And I beg to differ - in the strongest possible terms. You've misjudged the sort of person I am, deep down.

SO, YOU'RE A TOTALLY SAD BASTARD AND DON'T KNOW IT. WANT MY ADVICE?

I'M GOING TO TELL YOU, ANYWAY

But the market for books about the lottery looks all sewn up.

OH. SO YOU'RE A SMARTARSE, EH? WELL, DO YOU WANT TO KNOW WHAT YOU'D BETTER DO?

BUY SOME LOTTERY TICKETS

Yes

I've got 'em

No

No

No

Yes

Yes

No

Yes

HOW TO CONVINCE FOLKS YOU ARE RICH

If after you have attempted everything that you could possibly think of and you have still not won the lottery, then what are your alternatives? If you have explored every option known to man or woman and you are still skint, then I'm afraid you are just going to have to pretend that you have struck it lucky. This is not only relatively easy, but it also really upsets the neighbours.

Here are a few ways to convince folks you are rich without the benefit of money:

- Carpet your drive

- Hire a Ferrari for the day

- Boast about your weekend retreat
  (You don't have to admit it's a trailer tent)

- Order Caviar at the wet fish counter

- Have your slippers monogrammed

- Get a Stock brokers to send you their catalogues.

- Get a friend to call you at work, or at your neighbours, to leave an important message from the Sunday Times regarding the photo session for the UK Top 500 Richest Magazine.

HOW TO CONVINCE FOLKS YOU ARE RICH

- Hire a Butler or chauffeur or both.

- Name drop like mad, e.g., "I spent the evening with Phil & Liz"
  Whose to know that's what you call your ferrets.

- Change your first name to Sir.

HOW TO CONVINCE FOLKS YOU ARE RICH

- By selling all your possessions, and buying a mink coat.

- Stretch your skin, and selotape the excess behind your ears, so everyone will think you've had a face lift.

Cor she must be rich, even her knickers are furry.

HOW TO CONVINCE FOLKS YOU ARE RICH

- Have a family crest over your front door

- Disappear for long periods, and return with a sun tan.
  (This can be achieved by staying at your Mothers, and when the
  fancy takes you, using the solarium down at the local baths)

THE THINGS PEOPLE SAY WHEN THEY HAVE JUST WON THE LOTTERY

THE THINGS PEOPLE SAY WHEN THEY HAVE JUST WON THE LOTTERY

THE THINGS PEOPLE SAY WHEN THEY HAVE JUST WON THE LOTTERY

THE THINGS PEOPLE SAY WHEN THEY HAVE JUST WON THE LOTTERY

THE THINGS PEOPLE SAY WHEN THEY HAVE JUST WON THE LOTTERY

THE THINGS PEOPLE DO WHEN THEY HAVE JUST WON THE LOTTERY

THE CHANGES PEOPLE WANT WHEN THEY HAVE JUST WON THE LOTTERY

THE CHANGES PEOPLE WANT WHEN THEY HAVE JUST WON THE LOTTERY

THE IRISH LOTTERY WINNER

DIARY OF AN IRISH LOTTERY WINNER

DAY 1 – BUYS HIS FIRST EVER TELEPHONE.

In anticipation of the riches that will arrive, he has installed at his humble two-up-two-down, the first telephone he's ever owned.

Soon after the BT engineer leaves, he gets his first call:

Dring Dring...............Dring Dring

"Hello, this is Pat, Can I help you?"

"That's not John, then?"

"No, it's Pat"

"Oh, I must have the wrong number. Sorry to have disturbed you."

"That's all right, the phone was ringing anyway."

DAY 2 – TAKES DELIVERY OF FIRST CONSIGNMENT OF CASH. £1 MILLION IN £5 NOTES.

His wife insists he counts it all to make sure he hasn't been diddled.

Reluctantly – for he is a man of leisure now – he pulls a wad of notes off the top of the huge pile and starts checking, "5, 10, 15, 20, 25..." He he gets as far as 50, then stops, throws the wad back onto the pile and says to his wife,

There y'are, are you satisfied now? If it's alright so far, it's sure to be alright all the way.

Of course, she isn't satisfied, and makes him count the lot so, the next day,

DAY 3 – GETS NEW WIFE (A YOUNG BLONDE) AND A HUGE NEW HOUSE WITH A SWIMMING POOL.

sadly, there is a mirror on the bottom of the pool, and the blonde drowns herself.

DIARY OF AN IRISH LOTTERY WINNER

DAY 4 – NOW IN A MORBID FRAME OF MIND, STARTS WORRYING
ABOUT THE STATISTICS HE'S HEARD ABOUT THE LOTTERY.
One figure particularly worries him:
There is 5,000 times more chance of dying in any one week than
winning the Lottery.

DAY 5 – STILL WORRIED, STARTED TO THINK DEEPLY ABOUT
LIFE, BUT UNABLE TO FATHOM ANY OF ITS MYSTERIES.
Should a donkey with three legs be called a Wonkey?
Why does monosyllabic have so many syllables, and why is the
word "abbreviation" so long?
Are there any other words for thesaurus, and why isn't phonetic
spelt the way it sounds?
What would a chair look like, if our knees bent the other way?

DAY 6 – TO FORGET HIS WORRIES, HE GOES OUT DRINKING
AND SEEKING THE COMPANY OF WOMEN.
He ends up in a pub far from home. When last orders are called
he leaves, in the company of a lady he met for the first time last
evening, nearly falling over two drunks sat on the pavement
talking.
One says, "Look at that, the sun's up already"
The second said "You're drunk, that's the moon, and I'll prove it"
He says to Pat, "Is that the sun or the moon?"
Pat says, "How should I know, I don't live around here."

DAY 7 – IN POLICE CUSTODY.
Pat arrested, accused of rape by the woman he picked up the
previous evening in the pub.
At the police station, he stands in an identity parade. As his
accuser stops in front of him, he shouts. "That's her!! I'd
recognise her anywhere."

ALTERNATIVES TO WINNING THE LOTTERY

There are many alternatives you could try. The following is not one we
recommend, at least not without a GOOD DISGUISE.

Willy analysed the odds,
He was a real go-getta.
Who thought the draw was rather poor,
There must be something better.

He had a plan (the nasty man!)
To rob the local store;
That sold the magic tickets
That might stop us being poor.

Disguise was all important,
And he had the perfect ruse;
To dress in motorcycle gear,
From helmet to his shoes.

"Hand your takings over."
Said our Willy with a scowl.
It was a sinful, nasty act,
Immoral and quite foul.

He took the cash and scampered,
But it was a stupid stunt,
He had his name emblazoned,
Right across his helmet front.

CHOOSE A GOOD DISGUISE

ALTERNATIVES TO WINNING THE LOTTERY

You could try North Sea drilling...On a smaller scale of course.

ALTERNATIVES TO WINNING THE LOTTERY

You could always try to come up with a unique invention......A machine which will pick your lottery numbers for you could be a winner.

ALTERNATIVES TO WINNING THE LOTTERY

One alternative which could really be a winner, is to try and sell your family heirloom. Unfortunately, however, you need a to come from a special family.

Wicked Willy's cunning plan was charitable status,
To be an art, perhaps a sport; the winning apparatus,
To win the nation's favourite draw, and be quite rich for evermore;
And open up the rich man's door and much improve his status.

Perhaps a family heirloom purchased by a grateful nation;
Some diaries and old letters to provide some fascination;
And net a family fortune and the family name restore;
And bring a million quid at least to Wicked Willy's door.

He scoured the loft, the cellar for the archives to be sold,
And off to Sotheby's he went to turn the dust to gold.
But Willy's hopes were all in vain, he never did a fortune gain,
His dad was Private Willy Paine, and neither brave nor bold.

SELLING THE FAMILY HEIRLOOM

ALTERNATIVES TO WINNING THE LOTTERY

You could always try to cash in on the lottery ticket sales; but you must have a good trick up your sleeve.

PULLING THE PLUG & RESELLING TICKETS

It's greed that motivates them,
And it's greed that gives the chance -
To take the punters for a ride,
And lead a merry dance.

So Wicked Willie thought it through,
That punters rarely win;
It's those who run the lotteries,
Who really rake it in.

Clandestine and sneaky,
He spent a thousand quid,
To buy a thousand tickets,
Whereupon he deftly hid.

He caused an interruption,
In the village store's supply -
Of all electric power...
And you know the reason why!

He set his stall to sell them all,
To disappointed players;
Who keen to try prepared to buy,
At profits quite outrageous.

He sold the lot within the hour,
Before the power's commencement
Then sold the franchise to the scheme,
And doubled his investment.

DESPERATE ALTERNATIVES TO WINNING

You could always try getting more lottery tickets than you can afford. Unfortunately however, they are all computer coded.

DESPERATE ALTERNATIVES TO WINNING

You can wait for a wealthy relative to pass away.

IF ALL FAILS, JUST PRETEND YOU'VE WON

He dreamed of the day when good fortune,
Would arrive and then knock on his door;
He dreamed of excitement and riches,
Of yachts and rich friends by the score.

He thought he would put in some practice,
Get used to the perks and the joys;
So he told all that he'd won the jackpot,
And the night life he lived with the boys.

His friends multiplied by the dozen,
To toast his good luck and his health;
The presents and offers were many,
From the kind who would share in his wealth.

The word got around and they stood him,
For round after round given free,
And all of the beautiful ladies;
When asked were so quick to agree.

To share both their bed and their favours,
To share in the fortune and prize;
But soon they got cautious and knowing,
He had told them a whole string of lies.

He soon had to scamper, stay hidden,
From friends who were programmed to kill;
And daily he fears a Court Judgement -
From the ladies who send him the bill!

MAKING FRIENDS WITHOUT WINNING

BEGGING LETTERS / BEGGING YOUR PARDON.

Another thing that we hear quite a lot about in connection with the National Lottery is begging letters. we hear of lucky winners receiving thousands of the things, and stories of the Post Office sifting through them to save the winners trouble of coping with that amount of mail.

However what we are not told is the only thing that we would find remotely interesting, and that is how to write one and have it taken seriously....

Dear Sir please read my letter
I'm really on the skids
Hubby doesn't live with us
and I'm left with the kids.
I don't know how to manage,
It's really such a shame,
And I can't get the benefit,
I don't know how to claim.
So send me just a hundred grand
to help us to get by.
Wills & Harry need a break,
and I do too – Love Di.

BEGGING LETTERS

Of course you have no need to limit yourself to a small amount like a hundred grand, it may sound like a lot of money to you, but believe me to a lottery winner, this is just peanuts. However the secret is to convince them that you do not need the money but that it would give them a certain kudos to give it to you as in the letter on the opposite page, sent by my mate Di, who lives over the Co-op with her two Yorkies Wilbert and Harriatty.

To make your begging letter most effective, you need to select a theme, and work on it until it sounds convincing. There are a number of themes available, and here is a list of some of them:

1   Desperation for food, shelter and clothing for both yourself and your seven children.
2   Blackmail. This will only work if you know a secret about the winner, such as his name and address, or any skeletons he may have hidden in his cupboard.
3   Plea for friendship. You have to pretend that you are also a lottery winner, and that you sympathise with what he is going through. You plan how to win his/her heart and bingo, you have a rich spouse, who I am sure will forgive you for the little white lie.
4   A long lost cousin. Pretend to be a long lost cousin of his/hers. But not just an ordinary cousin, but one who saved the family from ruins, and one who is the reason why the winner is where he is.

READY MADE BEGGING LETTER TO A JACKPOT WINNER

Dearest Sweet Lottery Jackpot winner,

I understand through my mystic powers that you are going to be this weeks Jackpot Winner, so I thought I write now, and not waste time, so as to beat all the rest of the begging letters you are bound to receive, and also I wanted to talk to you before you won in case you changed to a measly selfish bastard.

Any way all I want to say is that I would like to have some of your winnings to pay off the loans I took out to buy the bleeding lottery tickets, which as this letter might imply, did not win.

I leave it to the goodness of your heart to decide how much to send me. I have to go now, because that tabloid newspaper guy is at the door again wanting to buy your name and address for £250 grand. He has got a cheek.

Yours waiting by the phone,

....

P.S. I was going to enclose a little celebration gift for you, but I had already sealed the envelope.

FINDING THE JACKPOT WINNERS

YOUR PRAYERS WILL BE ANSWERED, BUT.....

For spiritual guidance from a higher aural plane,
Old Ben confessed his poverty in language quite profane.
"Help me, Lord; to win the draw, the lottery of life;
Bring to me deliverance from trouble, woe and strife."

The weeks would pass but ne'er a word was sent from up on high,
Old Ben kneeled hands together as he looked up to the sky.
"Please, Lord! Oh don't abandon me, I really need that dough,
I'll thank you anyway I can, just tell me what you know."

Alas the guidance never came and desperation grew;
Old Ben prayed hard and frequently but how the weekends flew.
"Help me, Lord, I beg you! Help me win the draw;
And then a flash of lightening came and then the thunder's roar.

A voice boomed down, he heard the name
– the name it called was Ben;
He sat quite still and listened till it called his name again.
"I hear your nightly pleading" He heard the good lord say,
"But buy a ticket, Ben McRae and meet me half the way.

PRAYERS CAN WORK, BUT............

10 THINGS PEOPLE WOULD DO IF THEY WON THE NATIONAL LOTTERY JACKPOT

A recent survey was conducted amongst a fair mixture of social groups in a pub. to find out what would be the very first thing they would do, if they won the lottery jackpot. Here are the top ten:...

1 I would have plastic surgery to remove the grin.

2 I would tell my boss where to stick his job.

3 I would buy a round.

4 I would leave my wife.

5 I would tax the car.

6 I would go on holiday.

7 I would pay someone to have my hangovers.

8 I would buy the brewery.

9 I would have the kids adopted.

10 I would faint from the shock.

..........And for something a bit more daring; there is of course the Australian woman whose fiancé bought her a lottery ticket the week before they got married, and bingo, she won the jackpot. "I bet they had a good wedding" I hear you cry; well actually they didn't have a wedding at all – she left him a note saying she had always wanted to travel the world alone!!!

THINGS PEOPLE WOULD DO IF THEY WON THE LOTTERY JACKPOT.

Some people, would even stop hiding their winning lottery ticket, and actually tell the family of their good fortune. Do you have such a person in your family?

10 THINGS YOU HAVE ALWAYS WANTED TO KNOW ABOUT THE NATIONAL LOTTERY, BUT WERE TOO AFRAID TO ASK.

1. Who is that bloke who puts the balls in the machine, and how did he get the job.

2. Where do the audience come from every Saturday night.

3. Have they nothing better to do?

4. Why do they gasp every time a number drops out of the machine.

5. Does Anthea Turner buy a Lottery Ticket?

6. What are the odds against the numbers dropping consecutively E.g., 1, 2, 3, 4, 5, 6, Bonus number 7.

7. If you were lucky enough to get to push the button to start the machine, would you really have the nerve to display that plastic finger on your mantelpiece?

8. If the machine broke down, would the presenters have the balls to carry on?

9. Do jackpot winners continue to buy tickets every week?

10. Why Isn't Mystic Meg a Millionaire?

WHO ARE THE ALTERNATIVE GOOD CAUSES THE NATIONAL LOTTERY HAS HELPED

THE THINGS I FIND MOST ANNOYING ABOUT PEOPLE WHO BUY LOTTERY TICKETS.

1   When you see them marking their numbers on the slip. They do it so casually, and without any effort; whilst you know the traumas you went through calculating and selecting your numbers, as if you were taking part in brain surgery. These people shouldn't win, and indeed don't deserve to win, because they haven't sweated enough over selecting the numbers.

2   When you see someone buying loads of ticks at on time. Why should they have more chances of winning than me?

3   When they realise at 7.45 on a Saturday, that they haven't bought a ticket yet. they rush around like someone who has a hot rod stuck up his bum. I doubt whether they would get to the emergency and back in that speed if their arm was chopped off, or even their partner was having a heart attack.

4   The way some people talk, and pretend to be really kind and generous before their numbers come up. Promising equal shares for everyone they know; when you know fair well that once they win the jackpot, they will be struck down with a bad case of amnesia, not knowing anyone except the cashier at the travel agents.

5   People who pick their numbers through really outrageous methods, like how many times their dog licked his bum, or how many times he went for a pee. It's only a bloody lottery, not the end of the world.

THE THINGS I FIND MOST ANNOYING ABOUT PEOPLE WHO BUY LOTTERY TICKETS

6   When you are queuing up to buy your lottery ticket, and this
    moron is trying to look at the numbers you have so painstakingly
    selected.
    How much of a brain do you need to come up with six bloody
    numbers of your own?

HOW TO SPOT THE MALE LOTTERY WINNER

He doesn't feel the need to be nice anymore, so he suddenly starts ignoring his neighbours.

He buys a copy of Cheshire Life – to go house hunting, and takes the Times instead of the Sun.

He works when it suits him, daring the boss to challenge his lack of commitment.

He dumps his girlfriend, There'll be others at Cannes.

The Skoda is quietly replaced by a new Jag' and he is condescending about his neighbour's new Cavalier.

He has a permanent knowing smile on his mug.

Done for drink-driving he sneers and asks if the ban applies to Hawaii.

He gets a fax and a mobile, but doesn't need either.

He starts to take an interest in yachts and Mediterranean cruising.

He buys outrageous clothes more suited to a BBC arts programme producer.

He buys to brand Scotch.

He couldn't give a damn about environmental issues.

He feels and claims to be superior to Richard Branson.

He wonders if the win is sufficient to put him in the Sunday Times 'Richest 500'.

HOW TO SPOT THE FEMALE LOTTERY WINNER

She closes the door behind her quietly, and disappears.

She calls her boyfriend to tell him the good news.

She tells nobody – except the entire family no matter how remote.

She shops at the Supermarket – without bothering to look at the price labels.

She has her hair done – weekly.

She aches to tell the sniffy bitch over the road.

She becomes an authority on lip suction and tummy tucks.

For the first time in her life, she starts showing an interest in open-top sports cars.

She becomes less egalitarian, starts to speak up for the merits of public school and for the Tories too.

She becomes passionate about environmental issues.

She books an expensive holiday.

She orders a dozen credit cards....and uses them.

She goes shopping, shopping, shopping......

She says she can't make up her mind where to holiday; Rio Janerio or the Seychelles.

She orders printed stationery.

WHAT TO DO WITH YOUR OLD TICKETS

1 Send them to Good Causes with a note saying:
   " No 'thanks' necessary".

2 Send them to your bank manager with a note saying:
   " It's not as if I am not trying to find ways of paying back my loan".

3 Place an advert in an Irish Newspaper and resell them through
   direct mail. The advert should read:
   FOR SALE. POTENTIAL JACKPOT WINNING NUMBERS. ONE
   OWNER. ONLY A FEW WEEKS OLD. QUICK SALE, HENCE ONLY 80p
   EACH.

4 Send them to a jackpot winner with a note saying:
   "Enjoy my money!"

5 Put them in a photo album, so that your grandchildren can one
   day boast about how close the family came to being millionaires.

6 Send them to a paper recycling plant, and be contented with the
   thought that you helped to save the environment as well helping
   the Good Causes.

WHAT TO DO WITH YOUR OLD TICKETS

7   Light up a bum fire and keep your family warm.

SYNDICATES

Joining a syndicate at work, or at home is becoming very popular. You get the benefit of your syndicate member's luck, and more chances of winning.

Being a member of a syndicate is a blessing, and you must not forget those unfortunate people, such the self employed, who find it almost impossible to be a member of a syndicate, but at least they make an effort. A good example is Mr Jones, featured on the opposite page, who runs his own morgue single handed.

Did you hear about the guy who was talked into joining a syndicate at work. Reluctantly he accepted, as he thought this might give him the opportunity to get his own back on his colleagues who always outsmarted him. Four weeks after joining, the numbers came up for winnings of £6 million. But when he went to collect his share, realised that they had been pocketing the money and not bought tickets at all. Now Fred is suing them for the £4 he paid out.

The chosen lottery numbers of an Irish syndicate of three members:
7, 11, 31, 39, 42, 48   7, 11, 31, 39, 42, 48   7, 11, 31, 39, 42, 48

FIND AN HONEST SYNDICATE ORGANISER

WHO DESERVES TO WIN THE LOTTERY?

PICKING THE WINNING NUMBERS

By observing the winning numbers so far, one thing is very clear. The computer which picks the numbers is programmed to select the seven balls at random. The human brain is not programmed to do this very easily. Try to select six numbers at random from the 49 numbers in the box, and THEN read on.....

42	3	24	26	31	1	49
11	14	5	48	36	39	25
44	12	33	16	18	6	45
28	35	8	47	46	17	10
41	7	34	38	19	21	2
32	40	4	27	29	37	9
13	20	15	30	22	23	43

Why did you not pick the six numbers all from one line; instead you probably picked your six from various places in the box. This test proves that unless you programme your brain to think "random", your chances of winning are reduced.

REALLY CLEVER WAYS OF PICKING THE 6 JACKPOT WINNING NUMBERS

1   The numbers shown on the previous page have all been selected at random. There are 20 series of potential jackpot winning numbers on 20 straight lines of six numbers. If you decide to try these 20 numbers; and by some chance you do win the jackpot, just remember who gave you a hand when you needed it.

2   Position the square shown on the previous page on your watch. So that number 47 is dead on the centre of your watch. Next time you go to buy a lottery ticket, draw the position of the minute and the second hand on the square, at the precise moment you are about to buy your lottery ticket. The numbered boxes that the two hands cross are those numbers which you should choose, because it was fate that wanted you to be there at that precise moment.

3   Write the letters of the alphabet in the 49 boxes shown on the previous page, starting with letter A in the 42 box. Leave out the letters X and Z, and start again from A. The first series of the alphabet is for the Christian names, and second for the surnames. Choose 6 people that you love most, and write down the numbers on their initials. If this results in a win, make sure you give them their share!!!

THE WINNING NUMBERS SO FAR

DRAW DATE	WINNING NUMBERS	BONUS NUMBER
19.11.94	03 05 14 22 30 44	10
26.11.94	06 12 15 16 31 44	37
03.12.94	11 17 21 29 30 40	31
10.12.94	26 35 38 43 47 49	28
17.12.94	03 05 09 13 14 38	30
24.12.94	02 03 27 29 39 44	06
31.12.94	09 17 32 36 42 44	16
07.01.95	02 05 21 22 25 32	46
14.01.95	07 17 23 32 38 42	48
21.01.95	06 16 20 30 31 47	04
28.01.95	04 16 25 26 31 43	21
04.02.95	01 07 37 38 42 46	20
11.02.95	15 18 29 35 38 48	05
18.02.95	16 19 21 29 36 45	43
25.02.95	05 08 10 18 31 33	28
04.03.95	11 12 17 26 36 42	13
11.03.95	02 13 22 27 29 46	36
18.03.95	09 18 19 24 31 41	21
25.03.95	04 17 41 42 44 49	24
01.04.95	22 25 30 32 41 43	29

THE WINNING NUMBERS SO FAR

Date	Numbers						Bonus
08.04.95	14	17	22	24	42	47	34
15.04.95	01	04	06	23	26	49	08
22.04.95	08	18	20	33	36	38	46
29.04.95	09	15	22	31	34	48	23
06.05.95	05	14	17	35	43	48	22
13.05.95	07	16	25	26	28	41	19
20.05.95	15	16	17	28	32	46	22
27.05.95	12	13	25	37	44	45	09
03.06.95	01	21	29	31	32	40	27
10.06.95							
17.06.95							
24.06.95							
01.07.95							
08.07.95							
15.07.95							
22.07.95							
29.07.95							
05.08.95							
12.08.95							
19.08.95							
26.08.95							
02.09.95							

WINNING NUMBERS SO FAR ANALYSED

From the start of The National Lottery on 19.11.94 to 27.05.95 the following numbers have come up amongst the 6 winning numbers:

Number	has come up	times
1		3
2		3
3		3
4		3
5		5
6		3
7		3
8		2
9		4
10		1
11		2
12		3
13		3
14		4
15		4
16		6
17		8
18		4
19		2
20		2
21		4
22		6
23		2
24		2
25		5
26		5

WINNING NUMBERS SO FAR ANALYSED

Number 27	has come up	2	times
28		2
29		6
30		4
31		7
32		6
33		2
34		1
35		3
36		4
37		2
38		6
39		1
40		1
41		4
42		6
43		4
44		6
45		2
46		3
47		3
48		3
49		3

BRAIN TEASER FOR THE CLEVER NATIONAL LOTTERY PUNTER........

Using any of the numbers listed on the "Winning Numbers So Far" page, try to fill all the squares to show 12 series of winning numbers each on a straight line.

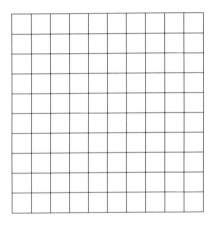

BRAIN TEASER FOR THE IDIOTIC
NATIONAL LOTTERY PUNTER.......

Using any one of the colours listed below, just colour the square.
Blue, red, green, black, blue, white, pink, purple, yellow and white.

THE SOCIETY
OF THE
VERY DESPERATE
NATIONAL LOTTERY
JACKPOT WINNERS-TO-BE

This is to certify that.. is a full member of the Society Of The Very Desperate National Lottery Jackpot Winners-To-Be; having attempted to win on numerous occasions, and has not even managed a prize of a Tenner.

It is with great pleasure that The President welcomes the new member, and offers unlimited access to the rehabilitation programme available at the club for such unfortunate National Lottery Punters.

Signed .... Date ....

On Behalf of The President

copies "100 CHAT UP LINES"
    ISBN: 1 871964 008 (128 pages A7) £1.99

copies "IDIOTS HANDBOOK OF LOVE & SEX"
    ISBN: 1 871964 083 (128 pages A7) £1.99

copies "10 GOLDEN RULES OF CHATTING UP"
    ISBN: 1 871964 091 (128 pages A7) £1.99

copies "SIZE ISN'T EVERYTHING"
    ISBN: 1 871964 121 (80 pages A7, free gift) £1.99

copies "THE 9 SECOND SEX MACHINE"
    ISBN: 1 871964 164 (80 pages A7, free gift) £1.99

copies "HOW TO WIN THE NATIONAL LOTTERY"
    ISBN: 1 871964 148 (80 pages A6) £1.99

copies "NOT WON THE LOTTERY YET THEN?"
    ISBN: 1 871964 156 (80 pages A6) £1.99

copies "SEX QUESTIONS & ANSWERS"
    ISBN: 1 871 964 172 (80 pages A6) £1.99

copies "HAVE YOU SEEN THE NOTICE BOARD?"
    ISBN: 1 871964 105 (80 pages A4) £3.99

copies "SEEN THE NEW NOTICE BOARD?"
    ISBN: 1 871964 180 (80 pages A4) £3.99

copies "SPORT FOR THE ELDERLY"
    ISBN: 1 871964 113 (48 pages A5) £2.50

copies "BEGINNERS GUIDE TO KISSING"
    ISBN: 1 871964 024 (64 pages A5) £2.50

copies "TIPS FOR A SUCCESSFUL MARRIAGE"
    ISBN: 1 871964 032 (64 pages A5) £2.50

copies "THE JOY OF FATHERHOOD"
    ISBN: 1 871964 040 (64 pages A5) £2.50

copies "OFFICE HANKY PANKY"
    ISBN: 1 871964 059 (64 pages A5) £2.50

copies "BODY LANGUAGE SEX SIGNALS"
    ISBN: 1 871964 067 (64 pages) £2.50

copies "WELL HUNG"
    ISBN: 1 871964 075 (96 pages A5) £2.99

copies "OF COURSE I LOVE YOU"
    ISBN: 1 871964 016 (96 pages A6) £1.99

I have enclosed a cheque/postal order for £ ....
made payable to IDEAS UNLIMITED (PUBLISHING)

Name: ....

Address: ....

....

....

....

County: .... Post Code: ....

Fill in the coupon above and send it with your payment to:

IDEAS UNLIMITED (PUBLISHING)

PO BOX 125

PORTSMOUTH

HAMPSHIRE

PO1 4PP

Postage FREE within the UK.

If you wish your purchase to be sent directly to someone else(e.g.;
Birthday, Christmas, Wedding, Valentines Gift), simply fill in their
name and address in the coupon above, and enclose your
cheque/postal order with your personal message or card, if desired.
We will be pleased to send your gift directly to your chosen recipient.